Poetry /

YOUNG WRITERS

THE INNER HURT

Edited by

Maria Chivers & Sarah Andrew

Cover idea by Robert Blanford (aged 13)
Cover design by Pete Morton

First published in Great Britain in 1996 by
POETRY NOW YOUNG WRITERS
1-2 Wainman Road, Woodston,
Peterborough, PE2 7BU

SB ISBN 1 86188 090 1

This book is dedicated to my sons, Jeremy and Mark and the tens of thousands of people who have Dyslexia/Specific Learning Difficulties.

Maria Chivers

A donation of fifteen per cent of the proceeds from the sale of this book will be divided between the British Dyslexia Association, Swindon Dyslexia Word Club and The Swindon Dyslexia Centre.

.

A simple definition of dyslexia is:

'Dyslexia means having difficulty with words in reading, spelling and writing - in spite of having normal intelligence and ability'.

Dr J E Cullis 1992

This book is written entirely by dyslexic children and therefore we have left all words as they were originally spelt.

Preface

During 'Dyslexia Awareness Week', in November 1995, I took the opportunity of organising a competition on Dyslexia - for all children up to 16 years of age. Information was sent to every school and playgroup in the Swindon area. My aim was to promote a greater understanding of dyslexia and how it affects people.

The contents of this book were written by children and in my view it is the greatest insight into dyslexia ever seen. It clearly shows the effect that dyslexia can have. It also shows the determination the children have in trying to overcome these difficulties - and not allowing something to keep them down.

Dyslexia affects four out of every ten people. Problems can show themselves in reading, writing, number work, short term memory, hand control and visual processing. Timekeeping, sense of direction and interpersonal skills can also be affected.

These difficulties often result in great frustration, bearing in mind that dyslectics are often of high or above average intelligence.

With the appropriate tuition and support students *can* reach their full potential.

Maria Chivers
Founder of The Swindon Dyslexia Centre

Foreword

My school days, on the whole, were very happy apart from the six months that I spent at a rather large, impersonal comprehensive school who judged everyone's ability on one exam that you took when entering school. At the grand old age of twelve, your fate was sealed. My parents, luckily, had the know-how and the resources to remove me from that school and send me to a direct grant convent school for girls, who recognised the problem and dealt with it.

I am not a severe dyslexic, otherwise I would not be able to perform the job I do. I was given the confidence at school to not worry too much about the things I couldn't do in life, but to work hard at the things I had a talent for - art, drama, dance etc. I always tell people that everyone has a talent and it's important to realise that and concentrate on the positive and aim to be the best at whatever they choose to do and everything else will follow.

by Anthea Turner

Contents

Ben Collins

Children Struggling on Reading

Children struggling on reading.
People straining on writing.
Words jumping up and down.
Running up and around.
It can not be - but it is!
An L jumping off a bridge!
I don't know how it can be.
But I hate being me.
(Only in a Dyslexia way)
How I feel when I get things right
I'm jumping with joy and there's not
a worry in sight!

Leigh Coxhead (11)

I'm Not Marking This Mess!

I can see his face ready to blow
he shouts so the whole class will know
Sir, Sir I'm stuck, I need more time
I told you what to do, don't step out of line

I find it hard and embarrassing with him yelling
about my reading writting and spelling
hurry up get on with it, I'm not marking this mess
I say, I need more time I'm doing my best

he tells me little kidds can do better than me
I've seen better from my daughter, she's only three
where's your full stops and capital letters
now go and sit down until you do better

It's hard to do my work I find
I never rest, it's always on my mind
then I get frustrated, rude and angry
because he doesn't understand me.

Mark Chivers (12)

Dyslexia is Worst for Me

Dyslexia is worst for me.
Oh it is.
It makes it a hard life.
It's not that I'm saying I'm backwards or -
dumb I've just got Dyslexia and that make
raeding, spelling.

Jenna Palmer (8)

It Gets in the Way

Dyslexia is bad it makes me feel sad
I am not glad just very very mad
It gets in the way eveyday
Why can't it go away
So I can go out and play?

Thomas Curson

Dislexia is . . .

Dislexia is . . .
Difficulty with spelling
Dislexia is . . .
Difficulty with direction
Dislexia is . . .
Blindness from words
Dislexia is . . .
Mixing up caplital letters and lower case letters
Having poor sense of time

Philip Hayward (8)

I Am A Bright Boy

I am a bright boy
some people will say,
But I have a problem that won't go
away,
When I pick up a book it's hard
for me,
To see the letters from B to D,
I know what I want to say but
sometimes I go the wrong way,
I need a bit of help and a little more
time, to write down on paper all the
correct lines,
It's been hard at times I have wanted to
cry and I have asked the reasons
why?
But I will get there in the end with
lots of help from my family and friends.

Luke Sheen (11)

Luke Sheen - Kingsdown School
Poetry Competition - Winner, Class 4

It's Hard

It's hard
when you can't read
It's hard
when you can't spell
Because you can't
Get your work done.
You have to stay in
When the others go out
And do extra time
To get your work done
It's hard.

I still like school,
I do lots of things
And if I keep on
Trying hard
I *will* get my work done
I love writing stories

Craig Ruggles (9)

Why When I Try?

I come to school.
I see all the other friends.
Who can rite and read.
But me, I'm all on my own
Not good at riteing.
Not good at reading.
I site on my bed,
I cry I cry and I cry.
But I boh't see why.
It's so hared for me.
Can't you see?

Jodie Cosgrave (11)

Dyslexia

Difficuty with spellings.
Yacht turns into yot.
Some member of a family has symptoms
Like turns into lik
Elephant turns into elifant.
Xylophone turns into xilofone.
Illness
Auditory and visiual difficulties of things.

Hannah Edwards (9)

What a Pain

What a pain
It gets on my nerves
I don't like talking about it.
I think I might get bullied if I told
someone.
I don't like thinking about it.
And I hope it goes away.

Daniel Neaves

Was I Thick, What Made Me Tick?

Was I thick? What made me tick?
I coudn't spell. I couldn't tell
the teacher what the word said
I tried so hard, was on my guard
But then one day hip hip harray the teacher said it's,
in your head
You've got dyslexia

James Ayre (11)

Dyslexia Looks Like Shoes on the Wrong Feet

Dyslexia looks like shoes on the wrong feet.
And feels like an embarassing moment.
It smells like burning toast.
Dyslexia tastes like sour sweets.
It sounds like a teacher saying
'see me!'

Lyndsay Peters (13)

There was a war in the pea bag
...then they made peace.

A piece
of pie

Christopher Lemaitre (9)

I Forget to Cross My T's

I forget to cross my T's and forget to put in my P's.
I have trouble reading or is it spelling. I dont know why it has to be me.
My spellings wobble, I try to put it right.
I know my a, b, c but when I come to it I forget x, y, z
I put it in the wrong place. It makes me do a horrid face.
My writing goes out of place. I feel like I'm going to space.

Christopher Lemaitre (9)

A Problem For Your Eyes

Dyslexia is sometimes a problem for your eyes.
You sometimes have problems with left and right.
Sometimes you have diffcuilties with your spellings.
Lots of people have dyslexia.
Eyes sometimes see the wrong things.
X-rays sometimes help people.
I had diffcuilties between left and right.
Adults can't sometimes spell things.

Hetal Patel (8)

At School it's Quite Hard to Spell

At school it's quile hard to spell,
but I can't wait for the bell at the
end of the day
Some people find it easy, some people find
it hard, some people take the mickey
but I don't care, so there!

Chris Bailey (12)

Is It Sad?

Is it sad?
Is it bad?
Does it annoy?
Is it fair?
Do people laugh?
Or do they care?
Are you thick?
Or are you not?

Phillip Banting

Dyslexia

Dylexia is horrible.
You see back-to-front.
Some times you loose direction.
Letters and numbers are hard to see.
Excellent brain thinkers have it sometimes.
X is very hard to write
I think that they will be angry because they can't see well.
And they feel very sad

Alison Roe (8)

A Word That Singles You Out

Dyslexia
A word that singles you out,
Makes you special,
Makes you different.

This word 'Dyslexia,'
Makes you spell things differently,
It swaps letters around in your head,
Makes nonsense sentences to muddle you up.

Dyslexia,
It groups you,
Puts a name on your forehead,
But never stops you.

This word 'Dyslexia,'
Helps you
Makes you stronger,
Makes you work harder,
It builds your confidence.

Kathryn Blanford (15)

Kathryn Blanford - Warneford School
Poetry Competition - Winner, Class 5

A World of Mistakes

I and I try.
But I can't see why,
I'me geting tould by my friends I can't right.
I get very lonley and trapped.
In a black houle.
Just when I get it right the teachers say 'Well done.'
But will I get it right next time?

Daniel Wheatley (10)

Dyslexia

Difficulties of all sorts
Yellow turns into yelo is
Spelling, confusion with
Left and right, direction.
Every day life is hard.
X is missing from the alphbet
I looks like L
And many other problems.

Sophie Knott (8)

My Mind is a Blank

My mind is a blank.
I go to school because I have to.
Lunchtime is best.
Teachers are okay.
PE is good because I don't need to use my brain.

Paul Duddridge (15)

I Am Better at Some Things Than Others

I am Dyslexic
some call me thick
and some call me names

I am better at some things
Than others
If I do something wrong
I ask teachers for help and they tell me.
I feel better now I now what Dyslexia is.

Ashley Wilson

Some People Think I Am Stupid

Some people think I am stupid.
Others think I don't care.
But to all of us who have dyslexia
Life seems totally unfair.

It doesn't matter how much I try
My hair is a mess, my shoes untied
My coat is undone, I spilt the tea
But at the end of the day I am still
only little old me.

I have to work much harder
to learn to read and write
but if you have this problem
don't give up without a fight.

Thank goodness there are people
who can help and understand
the plight of us dyslexics
because there are plenty of us around

Martyn Charity (11)

I Wonder Why

I wonder why, I do,
At these mistakes
It's like - I'm in big trouble
I'm mad if I do too much
I get mad
And when the teachers come to me, I wonder
'Will it be right?' Too bad
I feel like getting madder.

Craig Richards (10)

Louise Roberts (7)

I'm Dyslexic Dyslexic

I can see the sowlte sea.
I can see the moon.
I can see the poor people.
I feel hot.
I feel cold.
I feel bold.
But when I come to write it I just
can't becuse I am Dyslexic Dyslexic

Louise Maynard (10)

B/D's The Wrong Way Round

Dyslexia is when people get their b's d's the wrong way round.
You can get mums and dads with Dyslexia.
Some Dyslex people have spelling mistakes.
Learning is difficult for Dyslexia people.
Everyone with Dyslexia always fined it hard to work.
Xrays do not help.
I t hard for Dyslexia people to tell their left from their right.
Andrew is Dyslexic.

Andrew Deller (9)

The Mind of a Dyslexia Child

Where am I?
I am lost inside a world of letters and numbers
Where there are a lot of jumbles and squiggles
and as well lots of little symbols
That to me tell me nothink and I don't know why,
Sounds that don't mean much to me
And sometimes I lie awake in bed
Thinking, thinkinking what is this world of letters
that I and others don't understand
Is it just us alone, alone on a single stranded island
where no-one or nothink can be seen,
But just a big fog of numbers?
It is very fraustrating,
Like waiting in a room of black
with just a little spec of light
And as it gets brighter and brighter
And things become clearer to me
Now I see a world of numbers, letters and symbols
Of things that mean a lot more to me
And my future.

Gemma Gibbs (12)

When My Friends Could Choose a Book

When my two friends could chose a book
I was mad
Because I could not.
I was sad
when I have to write a story
I do not like it because I find it hard
And my friends say it is easy.
But I am having extra lessons
And it is helping me.

Melissa Ferting

I am Dyslexic

I am dyslexic.
It is hard.
I need help spelling.
And that's alright.

It is a pain,
not being able to spell.
It is a pain,
not being able to read.

I have it yes
but I'm alright
I won't give up
without a fight.

Nathan Miller (13)

Dyslexia

Dreadful to have,
You feel alone.
Slow to understand, why me?
Learning trapped, or so it feels.
Extraordinary me!
X or is it a cross, that's all I get.
I feel cursed, under a spell.
An awful thing to feel. *Help*!

Claire Sawyer (11)

Why Can't I Spell?

Why can't I spell a word?
Why does it come out wrong?
Why are there so many of them
In this whole wide world?
Why can't they be so simple
Just how I like them to be?
Why can't I spell that word?
I would really like to know.

answer is

I'm Dyslexic

Megan Robinson (11)

Cheryl Cox (7)

Cheryl Cox - Lawn Junior School
Colouring Competition - Winner

So Hard

Why me? Why me? I now I now
that I am the silly one. I
allwas get my d and b ronud
the wrong way. The teachers all
ways tell me. that I love to put
them riet. Don't you gust
see. That I find it so hard!

Lisa Kew (11)

Dyslexia

Difficulty with maths problems.
You can't spell very well when you write
Some difficulty in remembering patterens.
Left and right confuse you.
East and west get muddeled up.
X is one of the letters the can see
It means you have difficulty with rhythm.
A problem with maths symbols

Lauren Griffiths (9)

When I Found Out I Was Dyslexic

When I found awt I was dyslexic
I felt sad.
I cannat read or write very well but
I like having extra lessons
To help me to learn

Kylie Burt

Penalised

Lonely in a world where it seems no-one understands.
Struggle against something, you did not know you had until you were 10,
thinking you were thick, and put in bottom for everything.
Head Master at Junior School knew what was wrong,
but did not tell the parents. Mother finds out there's somethings wrong,
Head Master says, she not that bad Dyslexic, we don't want to
waste our money,
on her. From here on in, thought her Mother, it's going to be a struggle,
but somehow we will succeed.

I was in my last year at Junior School, glad to be leaving.
But there's a story, I have to tell you.
In class happy as could be, when the teacher, plucked me from my chair.
Showed me these cards, I could not read, nor spell, the words upon them.
She got so mad, she got so frustrated, as I was the one person,
she possibly could not teach, the problem she could not solve.

Some people think you put it on, that you have got a problem.
Also think, dyslexia, is a dirty word.
Are these people scared of the word, or something?
What do you think, if you are one of these people?
I had a teacher, who did not say, *Dyslexic*, but said, I had a bad
spelling problem,
it would be with me for the rest of my life!
Does a Dyslexic have a disease they don't want to catch,
no, again it is a case of the old problem, not enough money.
To them maybe, dyslexia, is some thing that they have to pay out
lots of money
which they need for other things, more valuable things than you.

Being dyslexic can also be very frustrating,
as you hand in work, that took you ages to write,
the teacher hands you back that piece of work, covered in red pen,
myself I can find it sole destroying.
How about you?

Carole Court (15)

Dyslexia is

Dyslexia is when you have problems
with writing.
Dyslexia is when you have difficulties
with numbers.
Dyslexia is when you get muddled
up with sequences.
Dyslexia is when you have difficulties
with rhythms.

Daniel Tredget (9)

Mnemonics - Vowels

*a*n
elephant
*i*n
orange
*u*nderwear

Matthew Burley

As I See it

I can see the
sun
I can see the
stars
I can see the
moon
I can see the
wold
But I just
Can't see
Lettres
The rit
Way arand.

Gemma Lambeth (10)

As I Watched the Teacher

As I watched the teacher come closer handing out the test,
I felt frightend, because everyone would find out sooner or later that
I have Dyslexia.
Do you care, have you a part
In the deepest emotions of my own heart?
I'm tired I'm fedup I need to escape
I feel like a globe, about to burst.
Dyslexia me I feel stupid why me?
I need some help but if I get some help everybody would say
Ha Ha you can't spell and read,
But I can read sometimes, but when it comes to spelling the words,
I go red I get hot and nerves.
Why me why do I have to have this Dyslexia.
There was an old lady who said to me
'Don't give up because deep inside you you know it's true,
Just find that spelling it's hiding in you.'

Charmaine Freeman (11)

Lost Time

When people say 'What time is it?'
I cover up my sleef
'Haven't got a watch' I say
don't want to tell them
I keep geting it wrong
Is it quarter *to* or quarter *past*?
Maybe soon I will know - at last.

Matthew Geraghty (10)

I Can Cycle

Hi I'm Michael
I can cycle
On a bike
I can do lost
of other things
But when I come
To writing
I can't get
The letters right

Michael Gleed

D is for Disappointment

D is for disapintment after tring so hard,
Y is for why, why and why
S is for sadness I sometimes feel,
L is for love and lafter, we all shaer,
E is for exsintment when I get it right,
X is for extr help that I sometimes need,
I is for I mening me,
A is for aferber and asers,

Claire Carter (9)

Claire Carter - Swindon Word Club
Poetry Competition - Winner, Class 3

I am Dyslexic, Sometimes I Feel Stupid

I am dyslexic sometimes I feel stupid
because I can't put as many lines down
as other people others do ten lins but I cannot
write that many at all.

James Doran (8)

English Sucks So Much

English sucks so much.
I feel as though I'm about to let go,
I hear the words that I know,
but when I get them down they don't make sense.
So I try to concentrate more and more,
but my pace slows down and I get real bored.
I stare out the window and glance at the sky,
I do so wish that I could fly.
I hear my teacher say 'speak up James',
This makes me feel so shy,
and at that moment I want to die.
I glance at her and she glares at me.
All I can see is her in a box!

James Wykeham-Martin (16)

The Spinning Mind

People read aloud in class
I wish it could be me.
I see the word in my head
But I can't say what I see.
Every time I try to read
It always comes out wrong.
I really want to read in class
I've waited for so long.
But I will keep on trying
I'll walk down my pier.
You know it's not my fault.
I've got *Dyslexia*.

Kate Fisher (12)

I Don't Know 15 From 51

I don't know 15 from 51.
I have difficulty spelling.
When I get it right it is dack to
front.
I can't tell left from right.
I can't spell things out like
Dys-lex-ia instead I spell things
out like this D-y-s-l-e-x-i-a.
Please don't laugh
But my dad has Dyslexia as well as me.

Rebecca Garth (9)

I Forget That I'm Dyslexic

I am dyslexic.
When I go to school I forget that I am dyslexic.
But when I get stuck I feel hopeless.
I was unhappy when I was on book 8 and
other people in my class was on higher books
than me.
I get excited when I get something right
I try hard at my work.
I find it difficult and hard doing my work.
My friends will help me along.

Patricia O'Riordan (13)

The Bell Rings, I Feel Worried

The bell rings I feel worried.
The teacher slams the door and shouts at us.
She shouts at me and Joe and some times at
James and David. Just then the bell
rings to go out. The teacher said
'Joe, Ben come here.' She shouted and shouted
as us, I didn't know what what we had
done wrong.
Dyslexia to me is sturggling in class.

Ben Collins (10)

Imagine You Cannot Read

Imagine you cannot read
You see the word
Then see a blur,
Then when people say, 'Read that.'
You reply, 'Oh . . . um . . . I forgot my specks.'

Imagine you cannot spell
You can say the word fine
Your reading's not too bad.
So when the teacher says, 'Spell that lad,'
You feel depressed, frustrated and mad.

Imagine having Dyslexia
You could get help and have helpful parents,
Or be left at the back of the classroom and be ignored.
And your parents don't bother either.
You think your useless,
But everyone is special in this world.

Oliver Wright (11)

The Inner Hurt

Micheal Larsson (7)

My Problem

I do not see properly because I
have dyslexia,
like 15 and 51 I find it hard to see,
I find it hard reading too.
Letters and numbers look different to me,
because as I said I have dyslexia.

Amelia Reed (8)

Teachers Think I Can't Be Bothered

Teachers think I can't be bothered,
but really it's because I struggle.
What I want to write is in my head,
but I just can't get it down on paper.
Some people think I'm stupid and thick,
but in the tests I get all the ticks!

Vincent Gallagher (15)

I Get Some Letter Mixed Up

I am dyslexic
I have difficulty
with my reading and writing.
I get some letters mixed up.
I have to work harder than other people.
But I have got used to it now.
I get more help.
I will get better.

Liam Lee

People Often Need to Get Help

Dyslexic people ofen need to get help, anybody
can be Dyslexic, children or adults.
They may need to learn how to spell, whrite and
read. I came to the Dyslexia Centre because I
needed a bit of help with somethings, my reading
and especially my spelling.
Dyslexia might mean to some people struggling
in class or what ever place you are at.

Alistair Clifford (12)

Difficulty With Spelling

You sometimes have problems with left and
right direction
Some people have eye problems.
Lots of people have Dyslexia.
Eyes sometimes see the wrong things
X-rays would not help
I had difficulties with my left and right
when I was seven
Adults sometimes can't spell words.

Kirsty Browning-Gower (8)

Sometimes You Want To Give In

I am dyzlexic
I get behind in work,
Every thing goes bananas,
I wish it woold go away,
other people treat you normally
But it isn't!
After a while you get used to it,
Sometimes you want to give in.

Jimmy D'Avila

Christopher Lemaitre

My Pen The Enemy

I'm fed up and lonle but I try
onist I do
I'm trapt in a wold of mistates
when my big grumpy old pen cumes out
I'm lost with out a hope in the world
A mustak! A mustak! So the teachers
seem to say
I wont to run away
and never see my pen again
'Why me?' I cry
I relly do try

Liam O'Neill (11)

I'm A Bit Clever

I'm a bit clever
some people will say,
But I have a small problem
That I want to go away.
When I pick up a pencil.
To copy my teacher's work,
I know it's right.
But when I write it down
it is all wrong!
I try my best to do it right.
But is just disappears out of sight.

Lucy Higgins

Understanding Dyslexia

Dyslexia is a word I didn't understand. Many people
pushed me aside.
But from the start, I knew I was different.
They called me careless and didn't try.
When really I was trying right from the start.
Spelling and words seemed to be getting worse.

Then people noticed I was trying but just not finding the
words on the page.
Now I understand as I am that, and finding it easier
through the days
as people are helping me on my way.

Fiona Sheen

I Find English Difficult

I find English diffircell because I find that the
assignments they give me are too hard.
Some times I do not hand my assignment in on time
because I find I get some spellings wrong.
The essays I get done I find that I get stuck on
the reading and spelling and I find that it is
very frustrating and I give up most of the time.
Most of the teachers give me a bit
more time to give my work in.

Garry Richardson

My Sister's a Bookworm

My sister's a book worm it feels like she got all the
reading brains,
she reads a book in just days.
But me I take months.
My mum says just 5 minutes reading it's beter than
arguing for 10 minutes.
And spelling it's just as bad.
I have to work harder than the other children.
They say that 'word' is easy to spell.
How can you manage to get it wrong?
But I can manage wiht some help.

Isabel Rowe

Dyslexia is a Puzzling Thing

Dyslexia is a puzzling thing, that
You should not be scared of it
Solve it
Let's do it together.
Expand your mind.
eXercise your brain.
I like it
And so will you

Richard Davis

The Inner Hurt

Kit Hawes (8)

It Gets on My Nerves

Dyslexia gets on my nerves.
Stops me doing things I like to do.
Please take Dyslexia away from me.
Oh, please, oh please, oh please, please, please!

Matthew Burley

Be Strong

Being Dyslexic it isn't fun,
Because people think that I am dumb.
They think I'm dumb because answas don't come
as quick as to some. I'm good at karate.
Nearly a black belt! I'm blinding at Rugby
A hooker and strong. But not as fast as
some. Being Dyslexic it's all right when
you get used to it.

My advice to people is be strong because the
answers don't come as quickir as to some.
It doesn't matter what people say. If you know
who you are accekt the peurson you are.

Andrew Shenton

I Can't Spell Very Well

I can't spell very well
But my reading's OK
I can't write fast
So I can't always keep up
But that's not really a problem.
I can't always write down
on paper what I mean
This can be a problem sometimes.

Dyslexia doesn't affect things
like drawing
which I do all the time
Or swimming and football
Which keep me in line.

Matthew Tydeman

I Feel Special

I feel special
Because no one else in
the class has Dyslexia.
People help me with my writing
I feel very very very happy.
My best friends Kica, Megane
Angela help me very much
I get neater.
They teach me the letters the right way
Not back to front.
My teacher helps me too.
They help me realise
How I can make other words.
My mum and dad are dyslexic
At least they used to be!

Samantha Ayres

Dyslexia Makes Things Hard

Reading and spelling easy for most
But difficult - for me
Others do not understand
Why it's different for me

And yet the other side of things
Are plain for me to see
While others ask me how things work
And how such things can be

Philip Derham

We Are Branded!

It's depressing
We're in lower groups for everything
And need extra tuition
And have to work super hard to keep up.
We have feelings of inadequacy
With a sapping of confidence.
Yet it's not always accepted as a reason
But can gain extra time for exams.

It's shrouded in secrecy
We are cast out and in the shadows,
Banished from the Right of Words
Outlanders! We are not accepted as others are,
It's like ME or Yuppie flu.
Telling teachers who aren't listening
It's like speaking but not being heard,
Being invisible, unable to explain it.

We try to prove things to our friends
But there is a barrier of words
Which is like a pane of glass
Or a flat wall for us and footholds for others.
They have a lift - we take the stairs!
We are in a race with a bunjee rope tied to us
Whilst our friends are without restraint.

We are like caged animals - others are free.

We are branded!

David Aiken & John Marchant

James Wykeham-Martin

When I Was at School

When I was at school
All those moons ago,
I thought that I was in another world.
I didn't understand
All those words in a book,
Nor could I spell them.
They jumped out at me,
I felt confused and abused,
But I had no-one to turn to.
Mum and Dad didn't understand
They smiled and held my hand,
But we fought a losing battle.

Now I'm 29 approaching 30
And quite looking forward to being thirty,
I'm not dazzled or confused
But I'm slightly amused.
I have a bit more work to do
Before I beat this problem of mine
And then everything will be fine.

Ben Parsons

Book List

Dyslexia - A Parents Survival Guide
by Christine Ostler
Published by Ammonite Books

Dyslexia at College
by T Miles
Published by Routledge

Dyslexia: How would I cope
by Ryden N
Published by Jessica Kingsley

Every Letter Counts
by Susan Hampshire
Published by Bantam Press

Growing Up with Dyslexia
by Margaret Newton
Published by NAMCW

Overcoming Dyslexia
by Beve Hornsby
Published by MacDonald and Co

This Book Doesn't Make Sense
by Jean Augur
Published by Bath Educational

Understanding Dyslexia
by T R Miles
Published by Amethyst Books

Useful Addresses

Swindon Dyslexia Centre

**134 MORRISON STREET
RODBOURNE
SWINDON
WILTSHIRE
SN2 2HD
TEL: (01793) 433967**

Tel: 01793 433967

Department for Education and Employment

Sanctuary Buildings
Great Smith Street
London
SW1P 3BT

Tel: 0171 925 5533
Fax: 0171 925 6986

The Dyslexia Institute

133 Gresham Road
Staines
Middlesex
TW18 2AJ

Tel: 01784 463851

Helen Arkell Dyslexia Centre

Frensham
Farnham
Surrey
GU10 3BW

Tel: 01252 792400

Bristol Dyslexia Centre

10 Upper Belgrave Road
Clifton
Bristol
BS8 2XH

Tel: 0117 9739405

Hornsbury International Centre

Glenshee Lodge
261 Trinity Road
London
SW18 3SN

Tel: 0181 874 1844

British Dyslexia Association

98 London Road
Reading
Berkshire
RG1 5AU

Tel: 01734 66 8271
Fax: 01734 35 1927